The Battle Off the Court

A Survivor Story

TIMOTHY KENDRICKS

authorHOUSE®

AuthorHouse™
1663 Liberty Drive
Bloomington, IN 47403
www.authorhouse.com
Phone: 1 (800) 839-8640

Published by AuthorHouse 05/06/2016

ISBN: 978-1-5246-0756-2 (sc)
ISBN: 978-1-5246-0754-8 (hc)
ISBN: 978-1-5246-0755-5 (e)

Library of Congress Control Number: 2016907371

Print information available on the last page.

Any people depicted in stock imagery provided by Thinkstock are models, and such images are being used for illustrative purposes only. Certain stock imagery © Thinkstock.

This book is printed on acid-free paper.

PREFACE

Statistics show that writing is one of the best relievers of stress, and even the Bible says, "Write it down and make it plain" (Habakkuk 2:2). Therefore my prayer is that as the words pour from my heart onto the pages, the stresses of my past situations will be released and all who read them will be touched.

My purpose in writing this book is to release the stresses of heartache and despair, which occurred during my diagnosis of cancer and my loss of the game of basketball. My goal is to get in touch with the readers through encouragement and show them that that the Lord always provides a way of escape during the trials and tribulations of life. After reading, I hope they will learn what I learned—that even though you can't see your way out of your situation, God has a better plan and purpose for your life. You only have to acknowledge Him through the good and the bad while continuously asking for His guidance.

I want the book to relate to teenagers especially. Most teenagers focus on becoming professional athletes and forget about the other side of being professional. They don't consider health complications or rejection coming into play as a hindrance of progress, as they were for me.

With so much going on in the world today, everyone—and I do mean everyone—needs some form of inspiration or sense of purpose. That is why I continuously thank God for giving me another chance at life and to continue in a sport that I love. I also thank Him for blessing me with a beautiful mother, who, although she was strict and hard at times, provided me with an incomparable sense of love and security. My mother played a big part in my life. She required her children to set goals and constantly stressed the importance of education.

Trust me; she would not have allowed me to play if my academic performance was not satisfactory. I also thank God for blessing me with a supportive family: A family that remained present during times of physical and mental need. A family that provided memorable moments through laughter and support. Without my mother, family, friends, and, most importantly, almighty God, I wouldn't have made it this far and I definitely wouldn't be on a platform heading toward success.

CONTENTS

I've missed more than nine thousand shots in my career. I've lost almost three hundred games. Twenty-six times, I've been trusted to take the game-winning shot and missed. I've failed over and over and over again in my life. And that is why I succeed.

—Michael Jordan

CHAPTER 1

•••••••••••••••••••••••••••••••••••

TRAINING

In life, we are not responsible for the cards that we are dealt; however, we are responsible for how we play them. If I had a choice, I definitely would have initially thrown in my hand. However, now I realize that everything that I went through had a purpose.

I am a native of Jackson, Mississippi, born and raised in the proverbial hood of "Doodaville," which is located in Hinds County. The neighborhood was running rampant with drugs, prostitution, homicides, burglaries, gang violence, and a number of other issues that were not conducive to the upbringing of a positive young man—*especially* a young man being raised in a single-parent home.

My mother, Lela Kendricks, worked constantly to provide a good life for her children, and I am forever in her debt. I am proud of her for doing a great job with all five of us and to my oldest sister, Michelle, for standing in while my mother was working. My mother and father separated when I was about eight years old, and after that, I did not see much of him. My oldest male relative, my cousin Donald Shoulders, took the role as the lead male in my life, and, especially since we were in Doodaville, I'm forever grateful that he did.

Donald really showed me the way. He guided me in various ways but one in particular stands out: he introduced me to the game of basketball. When he put that ball in my hand, something ignited within me. I finally felt a sense that I could escape from all of the stresses of my life, and if you don't believe that a nine-year-old could have stress, I strongly encourage you to think again. Donald took me to the toughest courts in Jackson. Two that I distinctly remember are Lake Hico and Battlefield Park. These are etched in my brain because the OGs and thugs played there. Playing basketball against people much older than me was among the scariest experiences of my life. Some of these guys had either just been released from jail or had been incarcerated at some point in their lives. Although I was somewhat afraid, I knew I had to suck it up. I really had no choice because before every game, Donald would tell me, "Lace your shoes up, and go to work." In layman's terms, he was saying to be a man. After a few games, I was never afraid to play again.

I will never forget a moment when I was playing a pickup game with Donald. He threw me the ball, and, at the tender age of nine, playing against guys three times my age and twice my height, I scored the game-winning shot after coming off a screen. This instilled in me the strength of knowing that

I was able to overcome anything, and I am forever grateful to Donald for that.

Neither of us knew that I would later need this strength for what was about to come.

Whatever the mind of man can conceive
and believe, it can achieve.

—Napoleon Hill

CHAPTER 2

FIRST STREAM

Throughout the years, I lived, ate, and breathed the game of basketball. I was always good at a lot of sports, but basketball was always my thing. It relaxed my soul and eased my mind. The Almighty always provides a way of escape our situations, and I truly believed that basketball was my ticket for getting out of my 'hood.

Some of my role models in the NBA were Magic Johnson, Michael Jordan, and Kobe Bryant. I always tried to mimic their moves on the court.

Since I did not have a place to practice my newly acquired skills at home, I became innovative and built my own goal. I cut the bottom out of a bucket, and I nailed it and a wooden backboard to a tree. I did this because at the time, my mother could not afford a real one; however, I didn't mind. In the 'hood, we learned to adjust to our surroundings, especially when it came to playing street ball. Hell, I loved the game so much I would've played with a brick and a tire.

Coming from the game of street ball to an organized team was a bit of an adjustment. I played for the Jackson Bulldogs, and because I was the tallest guy on the team, I played center. Although organized basketball was fun, I had more fun in the backyards and parks because we could play almost how we wanted to. Yes, I said it, and yes, I meant it, but I knew that if I ever wanted to "be like Mike," that this would have to be my starting point.

I practiced day and night—in the morning with my team, at night with my bucket, and in the parks with my cousin Donald. I was indeed learning a lot from the organized team experience, but I wanted to stay true to my street-ball foundation. At this stage of the game, time was flying by so fast that I felt like an overnight success. I went from playing the center in the peewee league to playing shooting guard in middle school and with an AAU (Amateur Athletic Union) team named Branch West Reebok out of California. I felt comfortable at the position of shooting guard. I played so well that I started to receive recognition from several high school coaches. This increased my love for the game even more.

By the time I reached the ninth grade, I was the number-one freshman player in the state of Mississippi.

Since I had already made a name for myself, I knew that I had to come with my A-game every time. My goal was to be a freshman playing varsity. Although it didn't happen immediately, I was not discouraged. I waited patiently for my opportunity and played my ass off during the season. The ninth-grade season went on, and I was averaging around twenty-five points per game. Late in the season, Coach Herman Sanders finally noticed me and moved me up to varsity. I was thinking, *yes, I made it,* but I failed to realize I had to wait my turn.

I hated riding the pine. I can remember saying to myself, *Damn, Coach. I'm the number-one freshman in the state. Put me in!*

Well, one day the coach gave me my opportunity. He put me in as shooting guard. I was nervous but could hear Donald saying, "Lace up, and go to work." I played the position well and finished the season with high scores and the satisfaction of accomplishing my goal of playing varsity as a freshman. This multiplied my love for the game times ten!

Still high from the great season I had during my first year in high school, I carried that same intensity into my next summer in the AAU. During this summer, recruiters were interested in me, and I was actually receiving national rankings. Over the next years in high school, I felt like I couldn't be touched. I visualized myself as the player who could not be contained. Metaphorically, my goal was to kill the person defending me. I just felt, in the depths of my soul, that my next step would be the NBA. I was so dedicated to the sport that after every home game, I stayed behind to practice and wouldn't leave until they kicked me out.

A role as a leader came with the success of my game. Whatever I needed to do to help my team, I did. This included being an example both on and off the court. Being a leader off the court was not a problem, due to my strong desire to be successful. It was tough to get over on me or just tell me anything. I always told myself that the women would be there, and gangs, drugs, and alcohol were never my "thing." My faith in God kept me grounded, and the Holy Spirit continued to comfort me.

Because of my mother, I had a great foundation in church. My mother had us in church from Sunday to Wednesday—and more if it was a revival week. I went from school to practice and then straight to church at night. My mother always saw me working out early in the morning and late at night. She would always tell me, "Keep Him first in all that you do." I heard her and understood her, but honestly, with no real trials and tribulations, it went in one ear and out the other.

Little did I know that, very soon, these words would save my life.

Life is 10 percent what happens to me
and 90 percent of how I react to it.

—Charles Swindoll

CHAPTER 3

PERSONAL FOUL

During the next summer, I continued to play with the California Branch West Reebok team. We made it into a tournament in Las Vegas, Nevada, and let me tell you that I played the best that I had ever played in my life. This opportunity gave me the chance to show more coaches what I was able to do on the court.

After that summer, my mailbox was flooded with recruiting letters. The first was from the Georgetown Hoyas. I remember thinking, *Wow. A school that I watch on television is actually interested in me.* Over time, more and more letters came, and I could not believe that all of this was happening to me. My dreams were finally coming to fruition. For the first time, I actually thought that I could go to the NBA.

I was on a mental high going into my senior year, and I definitely wanted to go out with a bang. I wanted to show everyone the reward for hard work and determination. Since I was being highly recruited and doing well in football too, I felt that nothing could stop me.

Little did I know that I would soon be proven wrong.

During my last year of football, I played well despite football not being my primary focus. Everything was going well for me until around the fifth game of the season. While running for a touchdown, I received a low hit going into halftime. It was not what I considered to be a bad hit, but the pain would not go away. The trainers rushed me to the restroom across the field, where all I saw was blood. The blood was thick—and so was my fear because I didn't know what was happening. The hit must have caused damage to my kidney. My mother and brother immediately rushed me to the hospital. The doctors ran test after test after test, yet I was only told that it was a bladder infection and that it wasn't anything threatening or serious. They suggested that I leave samples of urine and said that they would continue to run tests.

While urinating, I saw that my urine was mixed with what looked like broken-down pieces of my kidney. All of this bad news was on my mind when I returned to the field. I finished the year out with the pain and didn't really worry because I could still move and perform at a high level. I just decided to tough it out until the season was over.

Football season ended, and basketball season was beginning. I missed the first two games, but when I returned to the court in game three of my final season, I knew that it was going to be very emotional for me. It was my senior year! My last time to shine! More importantly, I knew that I was going to sign with a *big* school.

The season started, and I didn't notice the drastic change in my physical condition until about mid-season. I began to lose weight. I would get very fatigued during the games and practices. I complained to my mother about the issue, and she once again took me to see the doctor. We went back and forth to the doctors, trying to get answers; looking for a remedy to whatever was going on inside of me—but we received no answers. I eventually returned to practice in hopes of closing out a spectacular high school career.

Our team made it into the tournament around Christmas time. During the first game of the tournament, I scored twenty-three points against Murrah High School. Since twenty-three was my favorite NBA player's number, I was "MJ" that night. I was on an emotional high. That is, until the second game. While playing in the second game, I felt as if my life was being sucked away from me. I could barely breathe, and I was afraid because this had never happened to me before.

My mother looked at me and in a stern voice said, *"We're going to get some answers."*

I attempted to stay strong for my mother, but I could see worry all over her face. When we arrived at the hospital, my mother made it clear that we were not leaving until we had answers for my condition. They ran more tests, just as they had done before. Only this time, unfortunately, we *would* get the answers to our questions. The tests showed that I had a massive tumor, the size of a football, over my left kidney. I immediately thought back to when I had blood in my urine during the football game. For a second, my life flashed before my eyes, and I thought it was over. However, looking at my mother as she began to cry, I knew I had to be strong for her.

We didn't know if the tumor was cancerous, and the medical staff wanted my family doctor, Dr. Don Gibson, to tell me the diagnosis. Okay, now I was nervous. I wondered, *what in the hell is going on?* The next day, my mother drove me to see our family doctor. Before we went in, I told myself to be tough and not to worry about the outcome.

Dr. Gibson initially wanted me to leave the room, but I refused. The doctor looked at my mother, who let him know that it was fine. At this point, he looked me in the eye and said, "Timothy, you have cancer, and it looks like it has spread to your lungs and your liver." He added that there was an 85 percent chance that I was not going live through this.

My mother began to cry, and it felt like every fiber of my being turned to glass and decided to crack simultaneously. It was if time had stopped. *I'm only eighteen years old! This is not supposed to be happening to me!*

I admit that I was thrown for a minute by the bad news but later got control and told myself that I refuse to play the victim. I learned early on that God has the final answer, and because of my faith, my life would be spared. Truth be told, I think I was more devastated hearing that I wouldn't be able to play my last year of high school basketball. My last time to shine was gone. This is what really hurt the most. I had worked and practiced so hard to be the best and was hurt that I wouldn't have the chance to really shine during my senior year.

During my battle, I wasn't really thinking about me. I remember being more concerned with thinking about how my family was going to make it. Ninety percent of my work and dedication to becoming an NBA player was for my family. Without the game, how was I going to give them a better life? I didn't know. I just knew that I had to—and that my work on this earth was not yet complete. I began to draw strength from my family, which gave me the courage to tell my cancer *game on! I have you; you don't have me.* Every morning, I would pray and repeat the words of my cousin, *lace up,* which in my mind is a trigger that there is a battle to be won; it tells me to do my best, and that's just what I chose to do.

CHAPTER 4

ZONE DEFENSE

I was later informed that this type of cancer occurred only in children. Therefore, we realized that I had this since I was a child. All of this time, it was growing inside of me, and my mother and I were none the wiser. The medical staff immediately began to take action. They informed me that I had stage IV cancer; if I had waited any longer, it would have been too late. Before I could receive any medications, I had to have surgery. I can remember thinking that this must be really bad.

One of the best and worst days I remember from when I was in the hospital was the day my teammates came to see me before a game. It was one of my best days because I loved my teammates, and the fact they cared enough to come to see me was priceless. It was the worst because I had to miss the game because of this stupid illness. Knowing that I was a major factor in getting our team to where we were but not being able to play was the biggest slap in the face ever. To make matters even worse, later that week a coach from San Diego State called; he had made plans to fly down to see me play. Regrettably, I had to inform him that I was ill and wouldn't be playing the remainder of the season. I informed him that I had cancer.

This devastated me because I never wanted anyone outside of the family to know. This damn cancer was robbing me of my dreams. The next day, reporters from the local paper (The Clarion Ledger) called, wanting to conduct an interview. When they confirmed that I was in the hospital, the story was in the paper the next day. While reading the article, I discovered that they had interviewed my teammates and coaches. I remember feeling vulnerable. This was not a good feeling to have. I was sick, and now everyone knew it. *How was I supposed to deal with this?* I'm not sure if stress caused my condition to worsen, however, I was once again told that I would die. The illness had once again begun to attack me physically. I stayed tired. I never wanted to eat, and I lost a lot of weight at a very rapid pace. I was initially around 203 pounds and had lost between seventy and eighty pounds.

At this point, I somewhat questioned my future. I can remember telling God, *I want to make it!* Talking to God always removed any and all doubt that I had. Mentally, finding out about the cancer had a small effect on me. However, I began to speak against it, consistently saying that I was cancer-free or that I was a survivor. This is what I had to tell myself in order for the healing in my mind to begin.

I knew that, no matter what happened with surgery or treatment, I would defeat this cancer. I wasn't going to allow this to get me down. I was not going to allow it to depress me. I was in complete authority and control. Now, what did have me depressed was the fact that I wasn't on the court playing. This always ran through my head. I was so anxious to get back out there on the court and would do anything to be there. I was secure in my faith, knowing that I would be playing again— in spite of what the doctors were telling me. Next to God and my family, basketball was my life. It was basically like a job to me, while I was growing up. I knew that it was my ticket to getting to the next level. This had been my dream ever since I was a child, and I wasn't about to let it go. The only thing I wanted to do was get to the NBA. I was used to going into battle *on* the court; now I would use my thirst for the game as inspiration and motivation to overcome this battle *off* the court.

After surgery, it was time for chemotherapy. I also had to have radiation treatments to shrink and eliminate tumors that had spread throughout my body. I endured weeks and weeks of long hours of chemo. The chemo of was so strong that if I tried to eat anything, I would immediately throw it up. Not to mention that the food had no taste. The medicine was horrible; as bad as the chemo. It only broke me down. Out of everything, the radiation had the worst effect on me. The medical staff used a laser that to burn right through my body to remove the cancerous spots from my organs. To stay positive, I had to relate my treatment to the game that I loved. I processed the painful times as being fouled on the court. Yeah, it hurt for a minute, but eventually I would get to shoot my free throws. Trust me—I didn't plan on missing.

Eighty percent of success is showing up.

—Woody Allen

CHAPTER 5

••••••••••••••••••••••••••••••••••

FULL COURT DEFENSE

I constantly reminded myself that giving up was not an option. My mother had always been there for me, and I refused not to be there for her. My mother only had a fifth-grade education on account of having had to assist in providing for her family. I was determined to ensure that her struggle was over. The mere thought of her struggling drove me to a speedy recovery and kept the vision of becoming a college graduate in front of me. I knew that it would bring joy to my mother to see me—or any of her children—walk across the stage and receive a college degree.

My high school graduation was drawing near, and I had every intention of walking across that stage. The doctors thought it would be a great motivational factor for me, especially since I had missed my senior prom. I was warned that it would be dangerous because, although I had been taking my meds, my immune system still wasn't strong enough. They let me know that there were risks of becoming ill with something more than just cancer because of my poor immune system. They encouraged me but also warned me to be careful. If it would have required me to walk across the stage in a bubble, then call me "bubble boy" because nothing was stopping me. My mother would see me receive my high school diploma. Achieving the goal of obtaining my diploma empowered me not to give up on life on or off the court.

I was surrounded by encouragement, especially from my cousin Donald. Although people judge him on his past, he remained a positive role model in my life. He frequently told me that I was going to make it and that I was going to overcome. He always stated that I would be the one to make it out of this place. Donald's faith in me remained with me throughout my recovery.

Dealing with this nightmare included frequent visits to the hospital to have tests run. It was almost too much for me to take. I was just ready for it to be over! After a year of enduring the battle, my prayer would finally be answered. I can remember it like it was yesterday. The doctor entered the hospital room as my mother and I were sitting, close together, waiting for the results from the CT scans that I had had earlier that morning. The doctor sat down and read the results: *Thank God* there were no signs or visible spots of cancer! All I could do was cry. I was so happy. I looked at my mother; all she could do was call out to the lord that I had been cured from this terrible disease. It was a blessing and miracle at the same time. After thanking God first and foremost, then the doctor, I showed my mother all of the love that I had for her. This woman never left my side while I was in battle. During this battle I was the star player. My mother was the coach, and the almighty God was owner of the team. He called all of the shots and paid the price for me to be healed, and I'm eternally grateful.

After all of the crying, praising God, and hugs, the first question I asked was when I could get back on the basketball court. I knew that the recruiting process was like a business. Every coach is trying to get the right business partner to help lead the team to a championship. Being fresh out of high school, I did not know the ins and outs of the business, so I got caught up. I can remember being so excited when I was playing well; now that I was getting better, I just knew that the recruiting letters would start flowing again. I knew that I would soon be playing at one of the big-league schools, possibly even on my favorite team, the Georgetown Hoyas. Unfortunately, the recruiting coaches evidently didn't believe God to be a healer like I did because I never heard from them again. That's when I truly understood the business of the game. They wanted

Tim at 100 percent not at 50 percent, 75 percent, or even 99.9 percent.

This rejection only became more motivation for me. I refused to allow anyone, including the doctors, recruiters, and coaches, to determine my fate. I knew that it was once again time to lace up. When the doctors told me that I was clear, I wasted no time getting back into the flow of things on the court. I was determined to get signed. I worked my ass off trying to get my game back. I was working to get better—good enough that a coach, any coach, at the community college or university level would give me a shot. My faith was sufficient to know that I would be healed from cancer; I had the same intense faith that I would get back on the court.

Time passed, and I finally got my shot—something that the doctors told me I would not be able to do again. I was recruited by the Marion Military Institute in Selma, Alabama. I enjoyed playing basketball there, and we made it into the Alabama Juco conference. This was a big accomplishment for me. You've got to understand that, no matter what level I was playing, this was something that I thought I would never do again. While playing at Marion Military Institute, I slowly began to learn the business of the game. Instead of solely focusing on the game and allowing it to use me, I began to use the game to obtain a free education. As my mother said, you can always fall back on your education. I began to receive letters again from coaches, and I connected with one coach in particular: Coach Struthers from Jackson State University, who stated that he was interested in having me come to JSU to play for the Mighty Tigers. Since I was from Jackson, I knew a lot about the Mighty Tiger team and the way they played, so eventually, I ended up returning to Jackson, Mississippi to attend Jackson State University. It felt great to be playing at a D-1 school. I had won this proverbial *battle off the court*. I didn't allow circumstances, situations, or other people to tell me where my finishing line for life would be. I made it because of my faith, I endured because of my vision, and I survived by the grace of God. I continued to focus on my academics as well. Not to say that I was a straight-A student, but nothing was stopping me from obtaining my degree. I majored in criminal justice and received my bachelor's degree on Saturday, May 5, 2013.

I defeated the odds. I did what they said couldn't be done. These two accomplishments are proof that words of Philippians 4:13 (I can do all things through Christ who strengthens me) are indeed factual. Nothing was going to stop me now. I possess the power, the vision, and the determination to go forth and do great work and let the world know what the *almighty creator* has done and will do for me. This battle off the court was over, and I came home with the *win,* so on to the next one.

You can never cross the ocean until you have
the courage to lose sight of the shore.

—Christopher Columbus

The most common way people give up their
power is by thinking they don't have any

—Alice Walker

CHAPTER 6

COACHING

I was a young athlete who understood the pressures and significance of my injury. That's because I had a strong mother who was praying that, no matter the circumstances, everything would be fine. Having my mother, along with other family members and friends, on my side strengthened my faith. Since then, my faith has remained at an all-time high. Most young athletes and younger teens, and even some adults, lack a solid support system—the very type of support system that I needed to battle an illness like cancer.

That's one of the major purposes for this book: to be a support system that will get readers through any obstacle or situation that may come their way. I want others to learn that, even when all else fails and you think it's over, it's not over; God has the last say over our futures. Since I was a student athlete, I've created ten survival guidelines to becoming a successful student athlete.

1. Keep God first!

With God, all things are possible. Any goal you set in life is achievable, as long as you put Him first. In placing God first in your life, you're able to overcome any obstacle, hindrance, or distraction that comes your way.

Your thoughts:

_____

_____

_____

_____

_____

2. Be humble

You're not in the NBA, NFL, or MLB just yet; however, a positive attitude will get you there. Remember: your attitude determines your aptitude.

Your thoughts:

_____

_____

_____

_____

_____

3. Be a leader

See yourself where you want to be, and work toward getting there through practicing and volunteering. Everything is a trainable moment. Be confident in your skill set, and don't let fear hinder you from leadership opportunities in all areas.

Your thoughts:

_____

_____

_____

_____

_____

4. Be responsible

No one but you is responsible for your career path. Be proactive, plan ahead, and work hard to get there.

Your thoughts:

_____

_____

_____

_____

_____

5. Be positive

In spite of what's going on, remain positive. If you aren't pleased with your current situation, make your current situation change through planning, patience, and action.

Your thoughts:

_____

_____

_____

_____

6. Stay healthy

Know your limits, and know that your mental, spiritual, and physical health are gifts from the Creator—and for athletes, they are the ticket to receiving a free education and a sustainable career in the professional athletic industry.

Your thoughts:

_____

_____

_____

_____

_____

7. Stay open-minded

Although you may have dreams of becoming a professional athlete, doctor, lawyer, etc., you must realize that His plans may be different from yours. Keep an open mind, and know that, at the end of the day, everything will work out in your favor.

Your thoughts:

_____

_____

_____

_____

_____

8. Stay out of trouble

Ask yourself: Is it worth it? Is it worth your future, your education, your career and possibly your freedom?

Your thoughts:

_____

_____

_____

_____

_____

9. Don't accept failure

Don't ever turn away from a goal just because you didn't achieve a certain expected outcome. Remember that, even if you achieve a goal, follow-up is key to making the success even better the next time.

Your thoughts:

_____

_____

_____

_____

_____

10. Never settle for being mediocre

Are you truly living or existing? Living means you're in pursuit of excellence in all areas of your life, not just the one that you're talented in. Dare to be different, and remember—practice makes perfect.

Your thoughts:

_____

_____

_____

_____

_____

CHAPTER 7

CHAMPIONSHIP

While I was in college, I was able to accept the fact that I wouldn't play the game at high level anymore. That was okay with me. All I wanted to gain for myself was another shot at life. People doubted me; they didn't think I had it anymore. I dealt with all the odds that could be thrown at me.

I can remember walking into the gym after practice one night, just sitting in the center of the court, and asking myself whether I really gave it my all in trying to battle my way back. That's when I finally understood that I wouldn't play the game after college. The lord really blessed me with the opportunity to come back and play the game of basketball. I knew at that moment, though, that he had something better for me. In silence, I took some time, gathered all of my thoughts, and realized that I wanted more from my life after basketball. I decided to continue my education.

Education was a big deal in my family. My mother couldn't express it more clearly: she knew that in times like this, when things happen, you need something to fall back on. She called it a *backup plan!*

I decided to return to school in pursuit of a master's degree in sports management—just like every athlete who didn't make it into the pros, I wanted to have a profession somewhere in the big office. That's my main focus now: to work as a sports agent or general manager of a professional team.

In this life, we have different paths to travel; that's mine. But yours could be something other than being a sports agent or general manager.

When I walked to class, I used to think to myself, *Man, I wish I could have another shot to prove that I could play in the NBA or go to the best D-1 school in the country.* But let's not get it wrong here: never dwell on your past and what you wish could happen for you. So I became more patient and never thought anything like that again. Being patient has allowed many avenues to open for me.

These new avenues include being a part of the fire service, being a leader to young people, and getting degrees that I never thought I would I get. Being patient has opened up success for me—not monetary success, but the success of life itself.

CHAPTER 8

• •

WON!

In this life, I tend to look at *Rule 1* as God, Family, and Passion.

With God, nothing is impossible. We all have battles, but we also have to remember that He is the head of this life that we live. With God, everything is possible. This thought, and actually living it out, made things come true. My *faith!* My faith won this championship for me.

Family: there is nothing like having the love from the people who matter most in our lives. Parents, brothers, sisters, aunts, uncles, and cousins: These are the people who helped me stay strong. They would tell me to always stay strong and believe in myself. My family was there when no one else was. I always remember this verse that my mother, Lela Kendricks, would show me: "For I can do everything through Christ, who gives me strength" (Philippians 4:13). This verse stuck with me during those years and still wears on me today. Family keeps you up when no one wants to have anything to do with you. Trust me; I know!

Passion: we define passion as a strong and barely controllable emotion. This comes up because we have to have the passion to go for what we want in this life. That's the only way we will be successful in what we do. We have to have passion for what we do. The passion is within you; use it. I did, and you can too!

There is only one rule, but three separate categories. I'm here to show you that these three categories stand as one. They kept me going when I felt like giving up; they helped me remember that there will be better days for me. It can happen for you too.

PHILLIPIANS 4:13

9/20/07

Mothers are the only ones obligated to love you;
from the rest of the world you had to earn it.

The moment that you give up is the
moment you let someone else win.

"Kobe Bryant"

Who didn't want to be like Mike?

I know I did.

Whose number 1. whose number 2,
and whose number 3

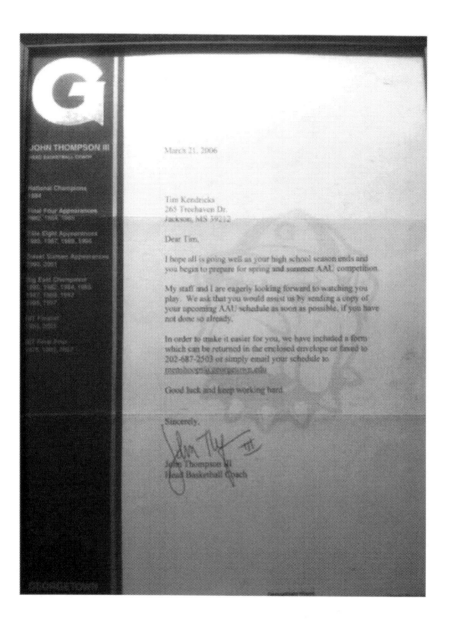

My first recruiting from Georgetown
Hoyas; that's when I knew I could play.

DETERMINED

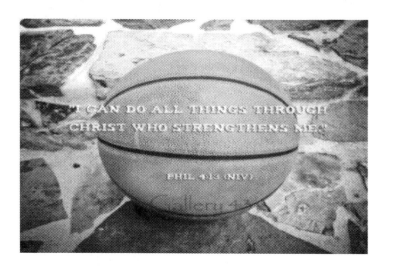

"I CAN DO ALL THINGS THROUGH CHRIST WHO STRENGTHENS ME"

PHIL 4:13 (NIV)

The game when I first learned that
I was diagnosed with cancer.

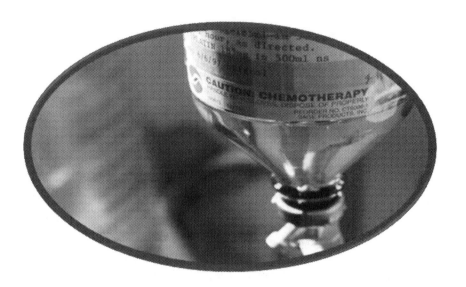

I didn't count the days.

I made the days count.

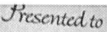

Presented to

Timothy Kendricks
Wingfield High School

For nomination to the

McDONALD'S ALL AMERICAN
HIGH SCHOOL BASKETBALL TEAM.

TIM KENDRICKS

Faith is to believe what you don't see; the
reward if thi8s faith is to see what you believe.

"Saint Augustine"

Where there is unity there is
always victory
FAMILY

RULE #1

GOD
FAMILY
YOUR PASSION

REFLECT ON SUCCESS!

Printed in the United States
By Bookmasters